THIS BOOK BELONGS TO:

ADAM

In the Bible, Adam is the very first person created by God. He was made from dust and placed in a beautiful garden called Eden. God gave Adam a special job to take care of the garden and all the animals. Adam also had a wife named Eve, who was made from one of his ribs. They lived happily in Eden, but one day they made a mistake by eating fruit from a tree that God had told them not to touch. Because of this mistake, they had to leave the garden, but God still loved them and promised to help them.

EVE

In the Bible, Eve is the first woman created by God. She was made from one of Adam's ribs to be his companion. Eve lived with Adam in the beautiful Garden of Eden, where they took care of the plants and animals. One day, Eve was tempted by a serpent to eat fruit from a tree that God had said not to eat from. She shared the fruit with Adam, and because of this, they had to leave the garden. Despite the trouble, God still loved them and cared for them.

CAIN

In the Bible, Cain is the first son of Adam and Eve. He was a farmer who grew crops. Cain had a younger brother named Abel, who was a shepherd. Cain and Abel both made offerings to God, but God was more pleased with Abel's offering. Feeling jealous and upset, Cain made a bad choice and hurt Abel. Because of this, Cain had to leave his home and wander the earth. Even though he made a big mistake, God still cared for Cain and marked him to keep him safe.

ABEL

In the Bible, Abel is the younger brother of Cain and the second son of Adam and Eve. Abel was a shepherd who took care of sheep, while Cain was a farmer who grew crops. Abel gave God a special offering from his best sheep, and God was very pleased with it. This made Cain jealous, and sadly, Cain hurt Abel. Abel's story teaches us about the importance of being kind and giving our best to God.

NOAH

In the Bible, Noah was a good man who loved and obeyed God. God told Noah to build a big boat called an ark because a great flood was coming to cover the earth. Noah gathered his family and two of every kind of animal to come on the ark with him. When the flood came, Noah, his family, and all the animals were safe inside the ark. After the flood, God promised to never flood the earth again and put a rainbow in the sky as a sign of His promise.

ABRAHAM

In the Bible, Abraham is a very special man who loved and trusted God. God made a big promise to Abraham: He would make Abraham the father of a great nation. Even though Abraham was very old and didn't have any children at the time, he believed God's promise. Abraham and his wife, Sarah, eventually had a son named Isaac. Abraham's faith and trust in God made him an important figure in the Bible, and he is remembered for his obedience and the special promise God made to him.

In the Bible, Rebecca is a kind woman who became the wife of Isaac. She was chosen by God to be a part of His special plan. When Abraham's servant came to find a wife for Isaac, Rebecca was very helpful and offered water to the servant and his camels. This act of kindness showed that she was the right person for Isaac. Rebecca and Isaac had two sons, Esau and Jacob. Rebecca is remembered for her kindness and for helping to fulfill God's plan for their family.

JUDAH

In the Bible, Judah was one of the twelve sons of Jacob and Leah. He was a leader among his brothers and played an important role in the family. Judah's story is known for his bravery and his role in helping to save his brother Joseph when the others wanted to hurt him. Later, Judah became the ancestor of a special family line that would lead to King David and eventually Jesus. Judah is remembered for his strong leadership and his important place in the Bible's history.

JOSEPH

In the Bible, Joseph was one of Jacob's twelve sons and was very loved by his father. He had a special coat of many colors, which made his brothers jealous. They sold Joseph as a slave, but he ended up in Egypt. Even though he faced many challenges, Joseph trusted God and became a powerful leader in Egypt. He used his new position to help people, including his own family when they needed food during a famine. Joseph's story shows how faith and kindness can help us through difficult times.

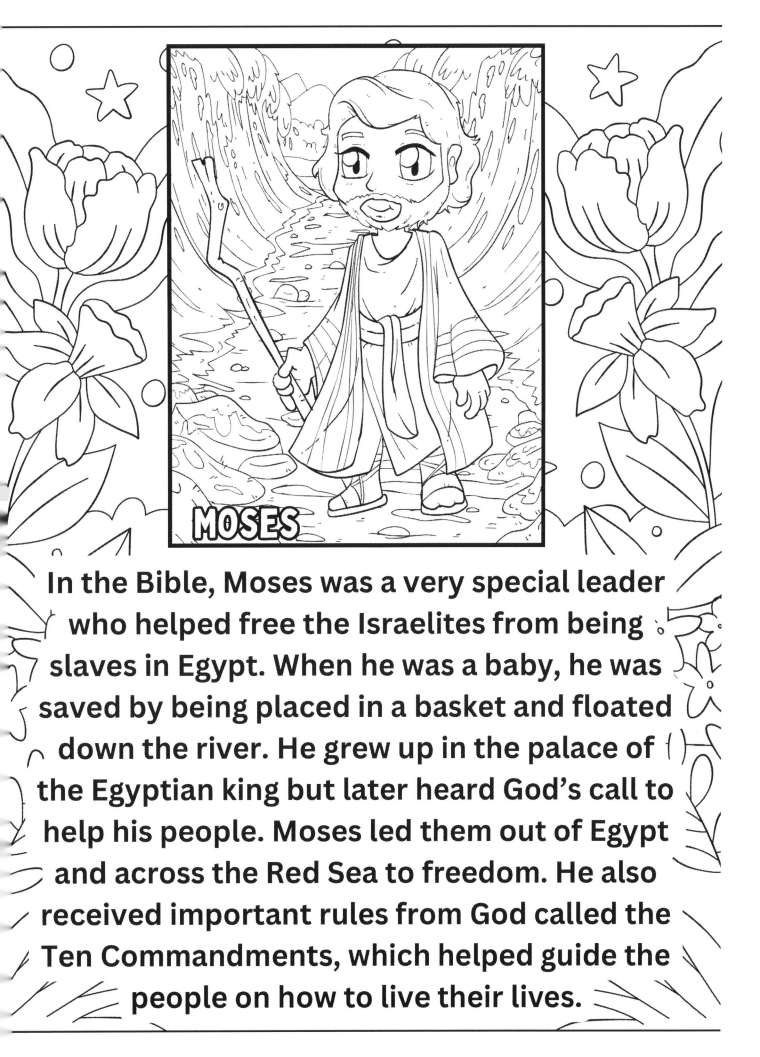

MOSES

In the Bible, Moses was a very special leader who helped free the Israelites from being slaves in Egypt. When he was a baby, he was saved by being placed in a basket and floated down the river. He grew up in the palace of the Egyptian king but later heard God's call to help his people. Moses led them out of Egypt and across the Red Sea to freedom. He also received important rules from God called the Ten Commandments, which helped guide the people on how to live their lives.

OLD MOSES

In the Bible, Moses with the tablets refers to the moment when Moses receives the Ten Commandments from God. According to the Book of Exodus, after leading the Israelites out of Egypt and into the desert, Moses climbs Mount Sinai where he meets with God.

AARON

In the Bible, Aaron was Moses' older brother and a helper in God's plan. He was a good speaker and helped Moses talk to the people. Aaron was also the first priest, which meant he helped with important religious duties and offered sacrifices to God. He stood by Moses during the time they led the Israelites out of Egypt and through the desert. Aaron is remembered for his support of Moses and his special role in leading and guiding the people.

MIRIAM

In the Bible, Miriam was the sister of Moses and Aaron. When Moses was a baby, Miriam helped by watching over him when he was placed in a basket on the river. Later, she played a big role in helping the Israelites escape from Egypt. Miriam was also a prophetess, which means she received messages from God. She led the women in singing and dancing to celebrate when the Israelites safely crossed the Red Sea. Miriam is remembered for her courage, leadership, and helping her family and people.

SAMSON

In the Bible, Samson was a very strong man chosen by God to help his people, the Israelites. He had super strength that came from his long hair, which he wasn't supposed to cut. Samson did amazing things, like tearing apart a lion with his bare hands and defeating many enemies of Israel. However, he was tricked by a woman named Delilah, who cut his hair and took away his strength. Despite this, Samson asked God for help one last time and used his strength to do a big act of bravery. Samson's story shows how strength and faith in God can help overcome challenges.

RUTH

In the Bible, Ruth was a kind and loving woman who chose to stay with her mother-in-law, Naomi, after her husband died. Even though she was from a different country, she decided to follow Naomi and take care of her. Ruth worked hard in the fields to provide for them and showed great loyalty and kindness. Because of her faithfulness, she later married a man named Boaz, and they had a son named Obed. Ruth's story teaches us about being loyal, loving, and taking care of others.

DAVID

In the Bible, David was a young shepherd who became a great king of Israel. He is famous for being very brave and for defeating a giant named Goliath with just a sling and a stone. David loved God very much and wrote many songs and poems that are in the Bible. He started as a shepherd, then became a king, and was known for being a good leader and a friend of God. David's story shows that even young people can do great things with God's help.

GOLIATH

In the Bible, Goliath was a giant warrior who was very tall and strong. He was from a group called the Philistines and challenged the Israelites to send out a warrior to fight him. Goliath was very confident and scared everyone with his size. But a young boy named David bravely stepped up and defeated Goliath with just a sling and a stone. Goliath's story shows that even the biggest challenges can be overcome with courage and faith.

JOB

In the Bible, Job was a very good and faithful man who loved God a lot. He had a lot of animals, land, and a big family. One day, Job faced many problems—his animals were lost, his children were gone, and he became very sick. Even though he was sad and in pain, Job still trusted and prayed to God. In the end, God helped Job and gave him even more blessings than before. Job's story teaches us about staying strong and trusting God, even when things are tough.

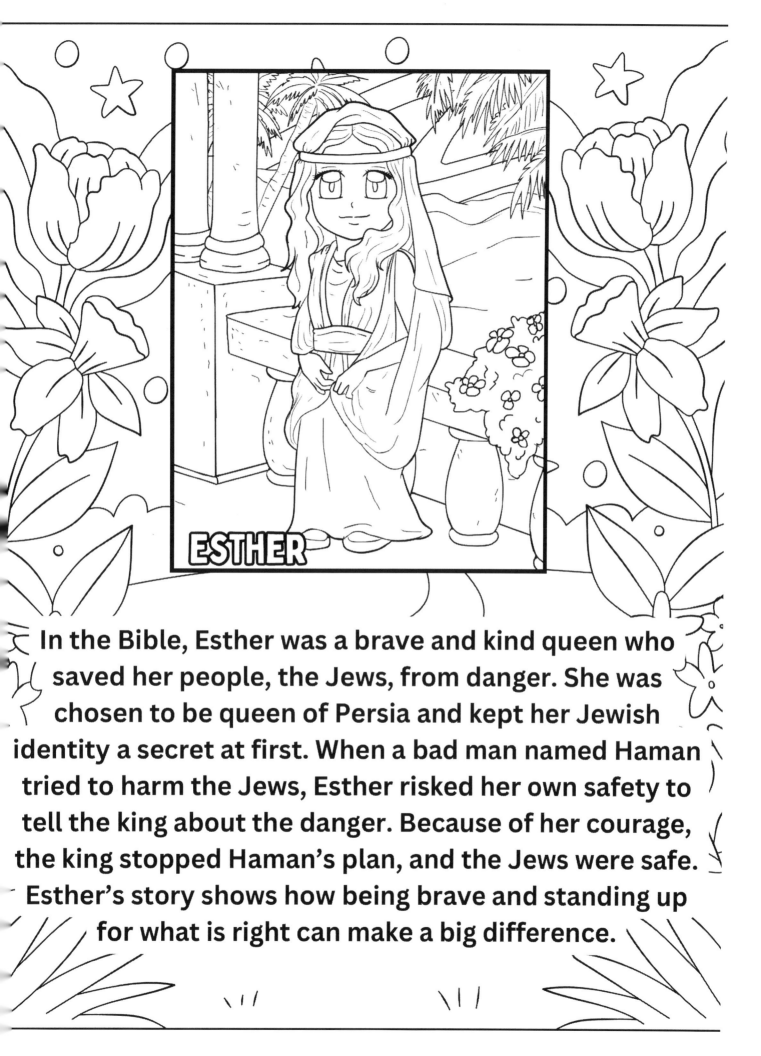

ESTHER

In the Bible, Esther was a brave and kind queen who saved her people, the Jews, from danger. She was chosen to be queen of Persia and kept her Jewish identity a secret at first. When a bad man named Haman tried to harm the Jews, Esther risked her own safety to tell the king about the danger. Because of her courage, the king stopped Haman's plan, and the Jews were safe. Esther's story shows how being brave and standing up for what is right can make a big difference.

DANIEL

In the Bible, Daniel was a young man who loved and trusted God. He was taken to a faraway land called Babylon, where he faced many challenges. Even when he was told not to pray to God, Daniel bravely continued to pray, and he was thrown into a den of hungry lions. But God protected Daniel, and the lions didn't hurt him. Daniel is known for his courage, faithfulness, and wisdom, and his story shows how trusting in God can help us through tough situations.

JONAH

n the Bible, Jonah was a prophet who was given a special message by God to deliver to a city called Nineveh. Jonah didn't want to go, so he tried to run away by sailing on a ship. But a big storm came, and Jonah was thrown into the sea, where a giant fish swallowed him. After three days, the fish spit Jonah out, and he decided to follow God's instructions. Jonah went to Nineveh and told the people to change their ways, and they listened and changed. Jonah's story teaches us about listening to God and doing what's right, even when it's hard.

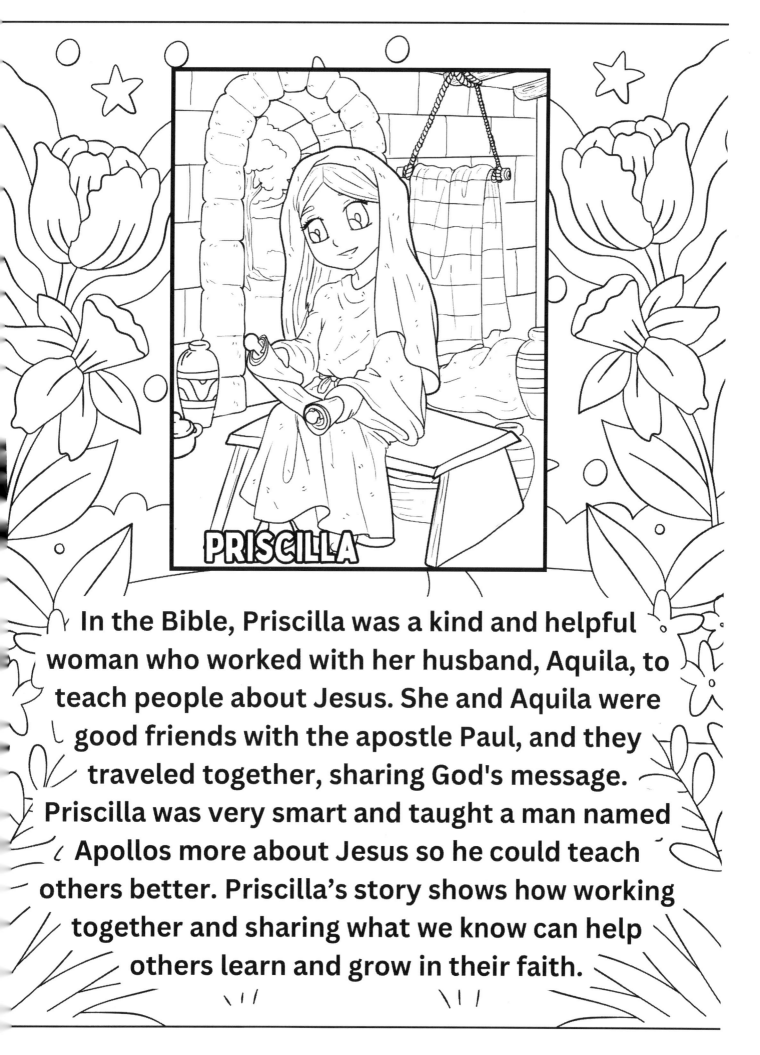

PRISCILLA

In the Bible, Priscilla was a kind and helpful woman who worked with her husband, Aquila, to teach people about Jesus. She and Aquila were good friends with the apostle Paul, and they traveled together, sharing God's message. Priscilla was very smart and taught a man named Apollos more about Jesus so he could teach others better. Priscilla's story shows how working together and sharing what we know can help others learn and grow in their faith.

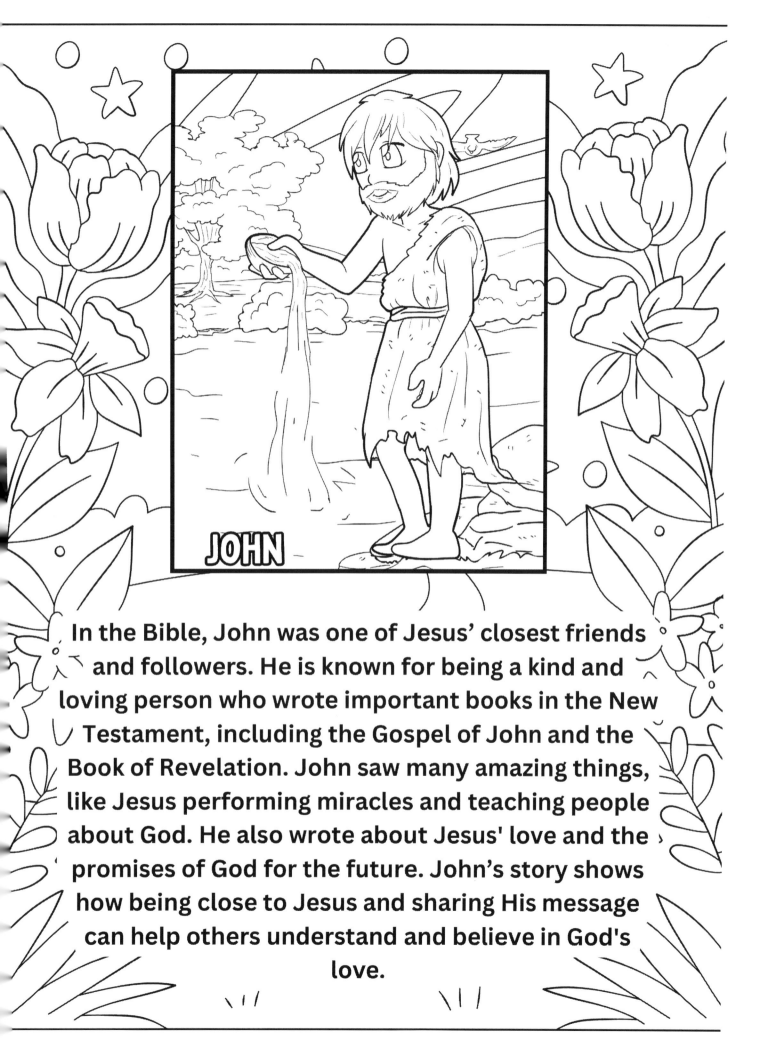

JOHN

In the Bible, John was one of Jesus' closest friends and followers. He is known for being a kind and loving person who wrote important books in the New Testament, including the Gospel of John and the Book of Revelation. John saw many amazing things, like Jesus performing miracles and teaching people about God. He also wrote about Jesus' love and the promises of God for the future. John's story shows how being close to Jesus and sharing His message can help others understand and believe in God's love.

JOSE

Joseph/Jose, the husband of Mary and the earthly father of Jesus. His story is primarily found in the Gospels of Matthew and Luke in the New Testament.

VIRGIN MARY

In the Bible, Virgin Mary is Jesus' mother. She was a good and kind lady who loved God a lot. An angel told her she would have a baby, even though she wasn't married yet. She listened to God and took care of baby Jesus.

Jesus is the Son of God and the Savior. According to the Bible, He was born to Mary, performed miracles, taught about love and forgiveness, and was crucified. He rose from the dead and offers salvation to everyone.

PAUL

In the Bible, Paul was a follower of Jesus who used to be called Saul. He traveled to many places telling people about Jesus and starting churches. He wrote letters to help and teach the early Christians. Paul was very brave and loved God a lot.

ANNA

In the Bible, Anna is a prophetess mentioned in the Gospel of Luke. She is an elderly woman who spent most of her life in the temple, praying and fasting. When baby Jesus was brought to the temple by his parents, Anna recognized him as the Messiah and thanked God. She's described as a devout and faithful woman who had a deep connection with God.

MARY MAGDALENE

In the Bible, Mary Magdalene is a special friend of Jesus. She loved Jesus a lot and followed him. She was one of the first people to see Jesus after he came back to life. Mary Magdalene is remembered for her faith and bravery.

REHAB

In the Bible, Rahab is a brave woman who helped the Israelites when they were about to enter the city of Jericho. She hid two Israelite spies in her house to protect them from the city's leaders. Because of her bravery and kindness, she and her family were kept safe when the city was taken. Rahab is remembered for her courage and for helping God's people.

Made in the USA
Coppell, TX
26 November 2024

41077212R10035